My Dad, My Rock

Victor
D.O. Santos

Anna Forlati

My Dad, My Rock

Written by: Victor Dias de Oliveira Santos
Illustrations: Anna Forlati
Layout: César Pires de Almeida

978-1-64962-122-1 (paperback)
978-1-64962-131-3 (hardcover)

City of Publication: Urbandale, IA, USA

Published by Linguacious®

www.linguacious.net
email: contact@linguacious.net

"Of all the titles I've been privileged to have,
'Dad' has always been the best."

- Ken Norton (professional boxer)

"Dad, was Grandpa a magician?"
"*Not that I know, my love.*"
"Then why did he disappear?"

I never met my grandpa.
And my grandpa never met my dad.

If I could meet my grandpa, this is what I would tell him.

My dad has two eyes, two arms and two legs, like most other dads.
But sometimes I think he has at least five of each.

Even when I am behind him, he always knows what I am doing.

If I let go of his hand, he always catches me. Sometimes I call him
Octopus Dad.

If I hurt myself, he runs to me faster than a monkey when it sees a
banana.

I sometimes climb on his back and pretend I'm on top of the world.
Nothing can hurt me up here.

My dad is my rock.

My dad likes being goofy with me, even if other people are watching.

He says those who laugh, joke, and love live longer.

He doesn't do everything for me. Instead, he shows me how to do it on my own.

Something about teaching a boy how to fish instead of always giving him the fish . . .

He always reads with me at bedtime. He says that a child without books is like a house with no windows.

When I am sad, he listens to me. Even if I cry a river, he is always there to wipe away my tears. And sometimes he cries with me.

He says some people say real men don't cry.

I think men who don't cry aren't real.

When I am angry, he asks me to count to ten. I am not sure why.

It always takes so long that when I am done, I don't even remember why I was counting . . .

When I can't sleep, he can't sleep either. It's as if he can feel what I'm feeling.

When he drops me off at school, we always hug.
He says hugs are food for the heart.

Sometimes I don't understand everything my dad
says.

He always believes in me and tells me I can achieve anything if I
try. He says I can be anything I want when I grow up.

When I grow up, I want to be like my dad. But with more hair, that's for sure.
My grandpa never met my dad, but I am sure he would be proud of him.

Just like my children will one day.